Dedication

I've been blessed to have a soul mate that pushes me toward my purpose. Micah Wainwright, I love you. You motivate me to do things I could never imagine. I'm excited that we get front row seats to each other's lives. Cheers to forever and more!

I would also like to give thanks to my loving mother, Earnestine Thomas, the perfect example of how a Christian woman should carry herself. I love you! Thank you for being the perfect parent.

Finally, I want to thank my supportive business partner, Tarah Coates, my true ride-or-die. Your encouragement fuels me. Thank you for being my rock.

TABLE OF CONTENTS

--Chapters--

INTRODUCTION

I would like to thank you for taking the time to purchase and read my book. It means everything to me!

This book will help you:

⭐ *Understand the fundamentals of determining and developing your goal.*

⭐ *Make the mindset adjustments necessary to reach your goal.*

⭐ *Strategize avenues to achieving your goal.*

Hope you enjoy!

Forget Your Fears

"My best advice to anyone that's starting a business is to forget all of your fears and just do it!"

Chapter 1

⭐ Franchon Parlour ⭐

After fifteen years of friendship, and a decade of professional hair experience, Jacinta Franchon and Tarah E merged goals to take their careers and talents to the next level. Early on, Jacinta and Tarah worked alongside each other at a salon Jacinta called home for most of her professional career.

Each recognized the other's passion for beauty branding and considering their current employment situations (which were not indicative of their evolution) they joined forces and launched Franchon Parlour.

Together, the rising entrepreneurs have enjoyed numerous successes working with other salons, local talent, and prominent figures in the hair and fashion industries.

Both women are proud and reassured of their decision to move forward together, but are also humbled by the outpouring of support from clients, colleges, and local talent, who have donated and bartered a plethora of services, from financial and legal to commercial real estate and artistic/media.

Relying heavily on their passion, professionalism, and ever-expanding skill-sets, Jacinta and Tarah's relentless work ethic and strong adherence to proven business principles, continues to pay huge dividends.

Franchon
PARLOUR
WHERE VINTAGE MEETS VISION

Chapter 2

⭐ About the Author ⭐

Jacinta "Franchon" Corum-Burgess (29) is a Maryland native and current co-owner of Franchon Parlour, a multicultural, upscale salon in Columbia, Maryland.

A 2011 Morgan State University graduate with a BA in Business, Jacinta is a twelve-year, hair industry veteran. Balancing two jobs with her numerous responsibilities as a member of her university's dance company helped to shape the rock-solid work ethic and passion for business that would lead her down the road of entrepreneurship to her status as a salon owner.

In 2012, while working as a stylist at a popular salon in Columbia, Maryland, Jacinta launched JFREMY.com, an online store for high quality virgin hair extensions, and within two years of its launch, the company saw profits of approximately $100,000.

A year later, in 2013, with JFREMY.com performing well, Jacinta sponsored an exclusive hair show tour that spanned Washington DC, New York City, and Atlanta Georgia.

In November, 2014, Jacinta started a new chapter in her career, when she founded the Franchon Parlour Salon with friend and colleague, Tarah Coates. Since the salon's opening, Jacinta's clientele alone stands at over 200 active clients, and continues to expand.

Aside from robust clientele growth, Franchon Parlour's launch brought with it, the opportunity to work with local talent and numerous hair/fashion gurus.

Some of the salon's most rewarding ventures include:

> Providing Hair and make up for the Mercedes-Benz New York Fashion Week, which featured Espion Atelier's Fall 2014 campaign.

> Creating customized JFREMY units for Ashley T. Moore and Cyn Santana's appearances on VH1's LOVE and HIP HOP Atlanta and New York respectively.

> Creating customized JFREMY units for Mamè Adjei and Justin Kim of America's Next Top Model Cycle 22.

Each amazing opportunity presented to Jacinta, happened because of her relentless work ethic, consistency, and perseverance. These traits have opened doors to such opportunities for Jacinta and Tarah as providing wedding hair services for former NFL running back, Ray Rice and his bride Janay Rice, as well as other NFL wives, such as Keisha McClain and Mrs. Smith.

Aside from accommodating a diverse spectrum of clients with varying stylistic needs, Jacinta has collaborated with Atlanta Housewives hair stylist, Sew Jodie, for celebrity hair classes. She also manages to carve out time to oversee published photo-shoots (Hype Magazine, Fox45, NBC, Voice of Hair, OWNtv, FMB magazine, Vibe Vixen, and EHOW.com style), land news castings, and network with photographers from all over the East Coast.

Helping clients achieve unique modes of self-expression through ever-evolving hair techniques is a practice Jacinta takes seriously, and hair weaves, precision cutting, and hair health are among her specialties.

Jacinta's extensive training background includes; Goldwell Systems, Design Essentials, Paul Mitchell Academy, Influence, Rusk, Wella, NY and Paul Digrigoli, and hands-on mentorships with some of the best Hairstylists in the industry.

Jacinta has an incredible eye for color, and her chic cutting and styling techniques make her a standout stylist with an elegant finishing touch.

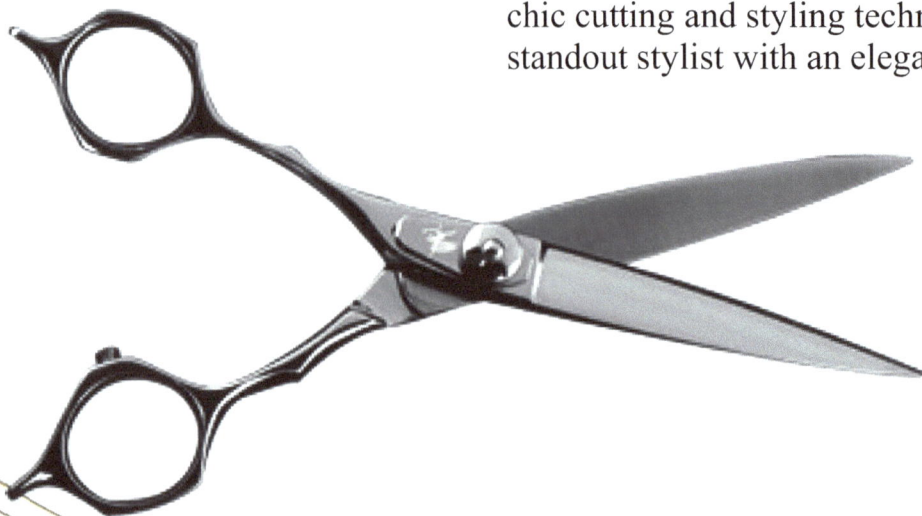

Passion

"Your passion is the key to your motivation, but consistency and determination to what you committed to is what will get you your success."

Chapter 3

⭐ Let's Start At The Beginning:Motivation ⭐

Motivation is vital, and varies from person to person. For some, kids and a secure future lights their motivational fires, while for others, money is key factor.

What is your ultimate motivation?

Define what makes you get up and go hard everyday.

Your 'why' should always mean more than your 'why not'.

Franchon Anecdote: *"In 2006, I decided to get my degree and my hair licenses at the same time. The fact that I would be a second-generation college graduate and the first entrepreneur in my family was my "why". It pushed me! I was also broke, so that was a motivating factor as well. You just wake up one day and decide! Make a decision, and make the sacrifices and life changes necessary to accomplish that goal."*

So, what is your why?

Chapter 4

⭐ Parlour Principles ⭐

Develop a clear and concise outline for your vision. What are your goals?

A goal is a desired result that a person or organization envisions and commits to achieve: a desired personal or organizational end-point in some sort of assumed development. Many people endeavor to reach goals within a finite time by setting deadlines.

In most cases, to get your long-term goals accomplished, you have to start with short-term goals. For every goal you have listed above, list a few short-term goals you can set to reach the long-term goal.

What are your current goals??

⬇

Franchon Tip: *"Perhaps you want to open a café in June of 2018. Your deadline to have the café open and fully operational is April of 2018, but in the year leading up to the overarching deadline, you must set smaller goals and deadlines for those goals as well."*

Franchon Anecdote: ": "A short-term goal I had before opening my salon was networking more. I decided to really develop a brand that people already new about before opening a location."*

What are your 3 year goals??

"The critical ingredient is getting off your butt and doing something. It's as simple as that. A lot of people have ideas, but there are few who decide to do something about them now. Not tomorrow. Not next week. But today, the true entrepreneur is a doer, not a dreamer."

Nolan Bushnell, Entrepreneur.

What are your 5 year goals??

Franchon Anecdote: "I was working at a salon as a stylist for almost ten years before I decided to branch off on to my own. The salon where I worked had the possibility of shutting down. I wasn't going to be without a job, so I had to make a move. In my heart, I knew I didn't want to rent a salon suite or work at another salon. I had my own brand, so I made a decision to partner with a like-minded individual and go own my own. I was never scared to branch off on my own -- I just didn't know where the money would come from! I prayed on it for weeks before I decided to just start looking for locations. God never gives you a dream that matches your budget. When you get out there and make moves toward your dreams, the universe has a way of celebrating that, and putting things in the right place at the right time."

Chapter 5

⭐ Questions To Ask Yourself ⭐

What is my mindset?

Do I want to become a millionaire?

Does my mindset match my work ethic or hustle?

What changes can I make to achieve my goals?

What is my master plan?

Am I being realistic about my goals?

Franchon Tip: *"Realistic thinking fits in with all of the other high priorities in my life. For example, my highest priorities are my faith, my family and my finances. To be rooted in my faith, I need to go to church, read, and meditate. For my family, I need to spend time with my man to be in a position to grow my family. For my finances, I'll always need to expand my brand and my business. That said, becoming a doctor is attainable for me. I certainly have the ability to go to medical school and become a doctor, but it isn't realistic. The time requirements would conflict with my higher priorities."*

What is my desired salary?

What is my daily goal to reach my long-term goal?

What is my weekly goal to reach my long-term goal?

What is my monthly goal to reach my long-term goal?

Franchon Tip: "Realistic thinking fits in with all of the other high priorities in my life. For example, my highest priorities are my faith, my family and my finances. To be rooted in my faith, I need to go to church, read, and meditate. For my family, I need to spend time with my man to be in a position to grow my family. For my finances, I'll always need to expand my brand and my business. That said, becoming a doctor is attainable for me. I certainly have the ability to go to medical school and become a doctor, but it isn't realistic. The time requirements would conflict with my higher priorities."

Chapter 6

⭐ Branding ⭐

When you are an entrepreneur you eat, breath and drink your brand 24/7. Many forget, ignore or fail to realize this. If there is a specific type of clientele you want to attract, you have to be that kind of clientele.

Always let your brand speak about you! Branding is neither true nor untrue. It is what it is. How you carry yourself, how you present yourself, and what your clients experience is your brand. Never present or project negativity.

Branding: **They speak about you**

Boasting: **You speak about you**

With branding also comes time management. Something to keep in mind is that every time you 'add time' you are wrong. Time is money! There is no time to waste time. If something is going to create more time, you must learn to be creative and get it done.

Franchon Tip: "If you are constantly discounting your prices, you will always have a clientele that is disloyal and only looking for a deal. You want loyal, professional clients, who respect your value. You also have to learn not to settle for less with your clientele due to your financial situation. In other words, do not cheapen your brand just because you need the money. Your client's financial situation is not your problem. Stand by your prices and fees."

"You lose your passion and become content when you wait".

There is an old saying -- "Good things come to those who wait." That is if those who work harder do not get it first.

The older we become sometimes, the more content we become with our money. We allow normalcy to take hold, become the standard, and convince ourselves this is how it is going to be. This is a stagnate mindset.

It is important to remember that we can always change our circumstances. One excellent technique is to develop the good habit of training our minds to do five things a day that move us closer to our short and long-term goals.

Franchon Anecdote: *"There were a lot of startup costs associated with my business. There wasn't one bank that would grant a loan to a salon. It's a cash based business. And because I couldn't get a traditional loan, I had to be creative because we needed the money like yesterday. So I did my research and applied for a merchant loan. A type of loan based on the potential revenue your business will bring in."*

You do not always need to change "what" you are doing, but you may need to change the "dose," meaning increase or decrease the frequency of the action based on what is necessary to accomplish the goal.

Overall, this means you must be willing to make major changes and sacrifices in order to see a desired change in your life.

What five tasks can you execute today?

1.

2.

3.

4.

5.

You do not always need to change "what" you are doing, but you may need to change the "dose," meaning increase or decrease the frequency of the action based on what is necessary to accomplish the goal.

Overall, this means you must be willing to make major changes and sacrifices in order to see a desired change in your life.

If you had one week to live, and you had a goal that you knew would be successful, what would it be?

List five goals you would want to accomplish.

1.

2.

3.

4.

5.

Franchon Anecdote: "When I decided to open my own salon, I never knew I was going to get it. I just new it was something that had to happen. So I physically got up everyday and literally began to look for locations."

What are some are your fears?

1.

2.

3.

4.

5.

What are the reasons you have not embarked on your dreams yet?

1.

2.

3.

4.

5.

Now that we have written it down, let's talk more about *FEAR.*

Franchon on Fear: "Fear has many sources and can take on many forms, but in an entrepreneurial context, it is anxiety caused by the possibility of failure in one form or another. Most people are afraid of things that are not accruing. Think about it. You are afraid of things that could happen. These are just thoughts!

As an entrepreneur, I have to overcome fear everyday, and literally tell myself I can do it. When I started my hairline in 2012, I had every fearful thought imaginable. What if I waste time and money? What if I don't find a location for my launch? What if nobody buys my hair? What if I'm not taken seriously? What if I can't afford a website? Literally every thought came to mind. I had to learn to stop thinking like that. At that time, I hadn't even started looking at hair yet!

It was silly. I had to change my way of thinking. The universe knows no limit! There is abundance for everyone.

"If you play with pennies you make pennies, if you play with dollars you make dollars. But if you play with millions you make millions."

Chapter 7

Change

Transactional Change
More of the same
5% to 50% improvement

Transactional Change is a process of modification intended to facilitate the attainment of strategic objectives by shifting functions, overall duties and specific assignments within a project or organization. Used in a business context, Transactional Change might describe the process of making constructive changes in such things as project requirements, product standards or reporting lines.

Transformational Change is an adjustment that is visible and you can see a difference! For example, if you want to be physically fit, and make serious positive changes to your exercise regimen (i.e., from once a week to everyday) and diet (replacing processed/junk foods with whole foods), you will see a startling difference in your body.

Transformational Change involves breakthroughs.
Albert Einstein once said, "Problems cannot be solved by the same level of thinking that created them."

A radical breakthrough in paradigms, beliefs and behavior, distinguishes Transformational Change, meaning you have to immerse yourself in things that connect to your goal to achieve it.

With Transformational Change, perceived obstacles may morph into opportunities, while seemingly irreconcilable opposites transform into creative tension, and change that seemed improbable or requiring long development may manifest quickly.

Steps for Transformational Change and Examples

1. Initial Idea: Ex: Franchon Parlour™
2. Idea Achieved: Ex: Franchon Parlour Salon™
3. New Idea: Ex: Parlour Pin-Ups & Parlour Pop-ups™
4. Repeat!   Ex: Parlour Marketing Work Book™

Franchon Anecdote: "When I decided to network more to brand myself, I attended additional classes to meet more professionals in my field. I posted samples on social media multiple times per day so people could always view fresh examples my work. I did photo shoots free until I was in a position to charge. I gave my clients the highest level of service I could. This process of Transactional Change played a major role in building my brand. Clients referred me to others because of the brand I created and the positive experience they had with me."

Chapter 8

⭐ Effective Ways to Market Yourself and/or Product ⭐

Facebook Ads: Ads can appear in News Feed on desktop, News Feed on mobile, and in the right column of Facebook on desktop. The platform may also pair Ad content with news about social actions that your friends have taken, such as liking a Page. Your friends might see news about the social actions you have taken in Facebook ads.

Applications: Create a conduit or system for collecting data from clients and potential clients. Use applications to keep them involved in your website.

Steps for Creating a Facebook Video Ad: Visual ads are very important. People often want to see the face behind the business and how you present yourself. First impressions are critical, so you must make sure it is a lasting impression.

- State who you are
- Explain what you offer
- Tell consumers why your product or service is useful or essential
- Provide information on how to acquire your offering
- Always request Name, Email, and Region

Credibility is an essential component in establishing relationships with potential clients. It leads to consumer confidence, which opens the door for you to educate clients about your product and/or service. It should noted, that no amount of credibility will impress or attract everyone, and that is OK, but without it, you are not likely to attract anyone.

Struggling is optional! Work is required! Learn to accept full responsibility for your life. (No more excuses)

Franchon Tip: "I use Constant Contact to give my clients updates on healthy hair tips, and to remind them to book their appointments through our salon website."

"Accountability is not a consequence. In order for it to become your competitive advantage, you must be willing to change what you expect from yourself and others".

~Sam Silverstein,
*No More Excuses: The Five Accountabilities
for Personal and Organizational Growth*

Chapter 9
Developing Effective Communications/ Speaking Skills

Use positive and powerful action words when communicating.

Positive Examples:

- ☑ Manifest
- ☑ Postulate
- ☑ Create

Avoid negative/counterproductive words when speaking:

Negative Examples:

- ☒ Try
- ☒ Hope
- ☒ Want

Never try. You do or you don't. That's it.

Hope is just another word for escape. You never hope. Just make it happen.

You do not need to want for anything. The universe does not understand that word, because there is an abundance of opportunity for everyone. Learn to keep the word want out your vocabulary. Just do!

Do not "umm" your way through verbal exchanges.

Avoid words like 'exhausted' and 'excuses'. Use powerful, effective words like 'powerful', 'improvement', and 'revolutionary'. These words uplift and radiate positivity.

Do not **CIRCLE** when speaking.

Circling is a bad communicative habit that entails going round and round, talking until you are blue in the face, never really answering the question or focusing on the topic.

If you can keep your focus, you can keep the dialogue on the track.

Do not allow your insecurities to pull you back to the same questions repeatedly. Teach yourself to ask the question and allow the answer.

Do not be afraid of silence.

The next time someone asks you a question, take a couple of seconds to pause and thank about what you want to say. This pause serves two important purposes:

- ⊙ It helps imbue the start of your response with confidence.
- ⊙ It eliminates the need to use filler words.

Pause. Think. Respond.

Chapter 10

⭐ Positive Energy ⭐

Reality> Vision> Structural Tension> Shift in Perception> Increased Perception.

The more positive energy you put into your goal, the greater the outcome. Everyday you need to put forth the effort to execute five actions that get you closer to your goal.

What are some actions you can implement monthly to reach your specific goal? Write down (and execute) your goals for each month to realize your long-term goal by the end of the year.

Month 1

Month 2

Month 3

Month 4

Month 5

Month 6

Month 7

Month 8

Month 9

Month 10

Month 11

Month 12

Chapter 11

⭐ FOCUS! DON'T OVER-BRAND YOURSELF ⭐

Pursuing multiple streams of income at once is a flawed strategy for novice entrepreneurs, because it erodes focus and is often a sign of FEAR (as discussed earlier). Focus on a specific goal, accomplish it, and then expand. Successful entrepreneurs tend to accomplish the initial goal before expanding into other areas.

Specialize or focus on a single product, service or market to establish initial success, then diversify to protect wealth. If you do not establish yourself in one area, how are you going to succeed in six? Solidify a "Core Competency" first! Make mistakes and grow.

Here are a few steps you can take to begin generating income in a single market:

- ✪ **PICK YOUR PATH**
- ✪ **EDUCATE YOURSELF**
- ✪ **GET A MENTOR, ASAP!**

Connecting with a mentor is a critical step, new entrepreneurs often neglect. It can be extremely difficult to navigate the waters of business without wisdom and guidance.

Find a mentor in your chosen field, craft or industry, and allow them to counsel you on the Dos and Don'ts.

I was able acquire my own mentor by simply finding someone that was more experienced and successful in my field, and asked if I could be their assistant and they accepted."

List Five People You Know or Have Access to, who could mentor you:

1.

2.

3.

4.

5.

Franchon Anecdote: "I've had many mentors over the years. I worked as an assistant to my very first mentor, John Lee. I shampooed his clients, cleaned stylist supplies, the bathrooms, and floors. I learned everything I could from him, before I went on to my next mentor, Kimberly. She educated me on the business and management sides of the salon industry.

GO TO CLASSES: Invest in your craft. Learn as much as you can, and master the essential tenets of your chosen industry. As your income grows, attend larger conferences and classes that are more advanced. The more you learn and network, the more opportunity will present itself to you.

READ: Many people make unnecessary mistakes simply because they will not read and study. There is a plethora of books in the informational sphere (Libraries, Book Stores, Internet, Amazon, etc.) that can provide you with step-by-step guidance in your field/industry of choice. Develop the habit of reading everyday.

WORK SMARTER NOT HARDER: Identify the skill-sets you need, form alliances with individuals who possess those skill-sets, and hire them to perform those tasks.

AFFILLIATE MARKETING: Join a program (send traffic to your program) and always retain a percentage of the sale. For example, attach your brand to a brand that is already established. You can always start by asking a brand if you can be a separate contractor to their brand.

UP BRANDING: Up branding is the strategy of achieving far higher brand recognition by aligning with someone whose brand has a higher profile.

MAKE MONEY AND MARKET: Launch 1-on-1 coaching, consulting, and other services.

"One deal, one time, to change your life forever"

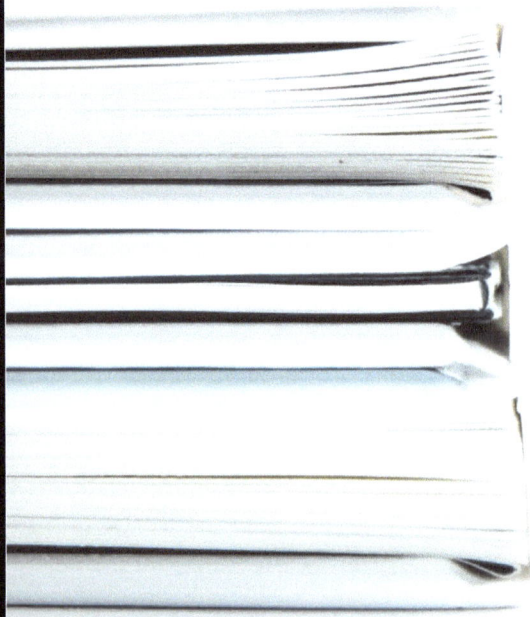

Franchon Anecdote: "When I opened my salon, I went through a thousand "no's" before I got to the one "yes" that got me the keys to my location. ***Don't be discouraged.*** There will be a lot of "no's" in your journey. But only you determine your outcome."

Chapter 12

⭐ Being Parlour Perfect! ⭐

Educate yourself

With the hair industry evolving constantly, education is the key to keeping up with the latest hair trends, clipper and shear style cutting techniques, colors, products, motivational speaking, and so much more.

When attending hair expos, shows, battles, etc., you will find many educational classes from professional barbers and stylists from all over the country (and even the world!) offering helpful tips. One of the most attractive aspects of these classes is that most of them are FREE!

After a weekend full of education and learning, you will return to your shop or salon, excited to share with your colleagues, all of the new tactics and techniques you can use to better your work and keep your clients happy.

Hair expos and shows are the best venues for picking up an assortment of items from tons of vendors from all over the country. From shear and clipper companies to product manufacturers, they are at these events! These shows serve as amazing outlets to make contacts in multiple arenas.

In addition, sample some of their wholesale products to consider selling in your shop or salon. This is a great way to obtain the best products on the market, which ensures keeping your clients happy and coming back for more!

"„,Education is the key"

"Your circumstances never matter.
It's all about what you will do next."

Chapter 13

⭐ The **Three** Tenets ⭐

1 Socializing

With social media having such an impact on today's world, barbers and stylists have a free platform to showcase what they have to offer. We have the opportunity to follow professionals who inspire us daily. The picture on the account may not be enough, however. Attending tradeshows gives us the chance to meet the face behind the profile and learn a vast amount from industry professionals. At these shows, friendships grow, businesses flourish, and we all get to share our passion for the same thing: hair.

2 Career Opportunities

As I said, we all have a passion for the hair industry. Why else would we have headed down this career path? I, myself, have been working behind the chair for over 16 years, and after attending my first tradeshow at Bronner Bros in Atlanta a few years back, it changed my outlook entirely!

I saw the opportunity to become more than just a stylist or barber working out of my salon or shop. Watching platform artists perform their artistry intrigued me, whether it was clipper cutting, amazing shear cutting, makeup, or just product promotion. Getting out of the daily hustle and bustle can be extremely healthy and valuable for excelling into different avenues in your career.

Who knows? You may get inspired enough to create your very own product line. All of these companies and vendors had to begin somewhere, and attending tradeshows is the best way to start.

Next time you receive an email or newsletter about a hair expo or show in your area, make the time to go and see what you are missing out in the hair world. I guarantee you will return with some extremely useful knowledge to really help your business grow.

3 Make the Time and Investment

If my words have not inspired you to attend a tradeshow, I am not sure what will.

When you walk back into work after visiting an event, you get an unexplainable feeling. Your positive energy will rub off on all of your employees, co-workers, and clients.

Between the knowledge, learning new techniques, meeting great people in your industry, or just picking up some new products you cannot wait use, this will be the ultimate hair recharge. In addition, we can all use a recharge from time to time. So, if you are in need of one, think about attending a tradeshow within the near future. Make the time and investment, and you can thank me later.

"Continuing your education in your field is important. It's a minimal requirement for your success."

Chapter 14

⭐ The Power of the Mind ⭐

"High energy produces higher income"

Many of us have a habit of focusing mainly on reasons why we cannot do something. When you say what you want it happens! So always, focus on the positive. Speak and seek positivity. Things you cannot control can often push out things that matter. Focus only on things that you should focus on. Do what matters and what you can control.

The power of writing the vision

Learn to write your vision and make a plan. As soon as your idea hits pen and paper, you are sewing energy into your vision. This underscores the five daily actions you can execute to sew into your dream. Write your vision first, and then take small steps each day to achieve it.

Writing down your vision is your initial act of faith. It is you solidifying ambitions revealed to you in your heart. Even if you do not quite understand it all, write it down anyway. Even if you cannot see how your vision is going to happen, write it down anyway. Your assignment is to believe what God has revealed to you through vision, and write it down. The "how" and the "when" is God's department. Just write it down!

Develop a plan…

Writing the vision down involves developing a plan. If you and I are going to prosper and succeed in life, we are going to need a plan, because if you fail to plan then you plan to fail. Writing down your vision gives you a tangible target to aim for. It is writing down what you want to happen. Taking your vision from your heart and transferring it onto paper is essential.

Engage in a 'Power Hour' each morning. Make plans, map out the day, and brainstorm. Unsuccessful people tend to stumble into and about their day. Successful individuals get up and know exactly what they need to focus on and accomplish.

If you attempt to do nothing you actually move backwards.

Spiritual Postulate: Is something that comes true in the physical because you think it, say it, and write it down. Self created truth. The minute you say it, it becomes true. It just has yet to happen in the physical universe.

SPIRITUAL LAWS TO LIVE BY

Get Rich

Build Relationships

Improve Health

Help Others

"The greatest discovery of my generation is that people can alter their lives by altering their attitudes." - William James

Franchon Tip: "Taking control of your attitude is a hard thing to do, but as soon as I took responsibility for and control over my attitude, I began to develop habits to have a better attitude. Happiness! It's a domino effect."

Chapter 15

⭐ Key Takeaway ⭐

Continued education is necessary if you want to master your craft. With new tools and products constantly coming into the marketplace, being knowledgeable of them will help you keep up with nonstop industry expansion.

Everyone loves picking up a new gadget, tool, or product, and the tradeshows have offerings that are not available at your local beauty supply store. Take full advantage when they come to your town.

Social media has been a huge platform that has been extremely beneficial to the hair industry and has added to its growth. It is a form of free advertisement offered to us, and connecting with your social media peers and colleagues can be a humbling, inspiring, and life-changing experience.

If you are looking to broaden your career, get out of your normal daily grind, and see what opportunities are appealing and available to you, let these companies know why they need you to represent them and their brand.

Chapter 16

The Hustle: Starting Your Brand

How to setup an LLC
Keeping overhead cost low

Find Help: With any business you need a mentor. Find someone that is more successful in your field and learn from their triumphs and mistakes. It will make your journey easier. In some instances, you may need a partner. Network and learn to work well with others. You do not have to do everything alone.

Finding Investors: Networking will help you find investors. Many potential investors just want to invest and collect a percentage. Allow yourself to be in situations where you can network with these people.

What to Keep on File: Knowing your customer always makes them want to come back, because they feel appreciated. Learn to keep a file on each client with full name, email and birthday. When special days or holidays come around you can send them a card or email them an e-card.

Product and Price Point: There should never be a reason why your customers do not know your price. Make your prices and products clear. Prices should not be different for different people or depending on how much you need to make that day.

Retaining your Customers: Clients are always attracted to businesses with "WOW" factors. I suggest having a customer service component that makes you stand out from other businesses in your field. One example a "WOW" factor I use, is giving my clients a care package of free hair samples for the Holidays. Another is on Valentine's Day, when my salon throws a Parlour Appreciation Party that features free food, DJ, and champagne!

Staying Connected to Your Clients and Consumer Base: Having a system that keeps your clients connected to your business outside of your service or product is important. Make it a point to have each of your clients email. You can send a monthly email blast providing updates on your business, as well as offers for the upcoming month.

Being the BEST in Your Market: Education is key! Make sure you take classes in your field consistently, and READ.

There is a lot of information out there, but many fail to develop the habit of reading, and as a result, miss critical information, such as advances in their industries.

Educate yourself in different areas by becoming a reader.

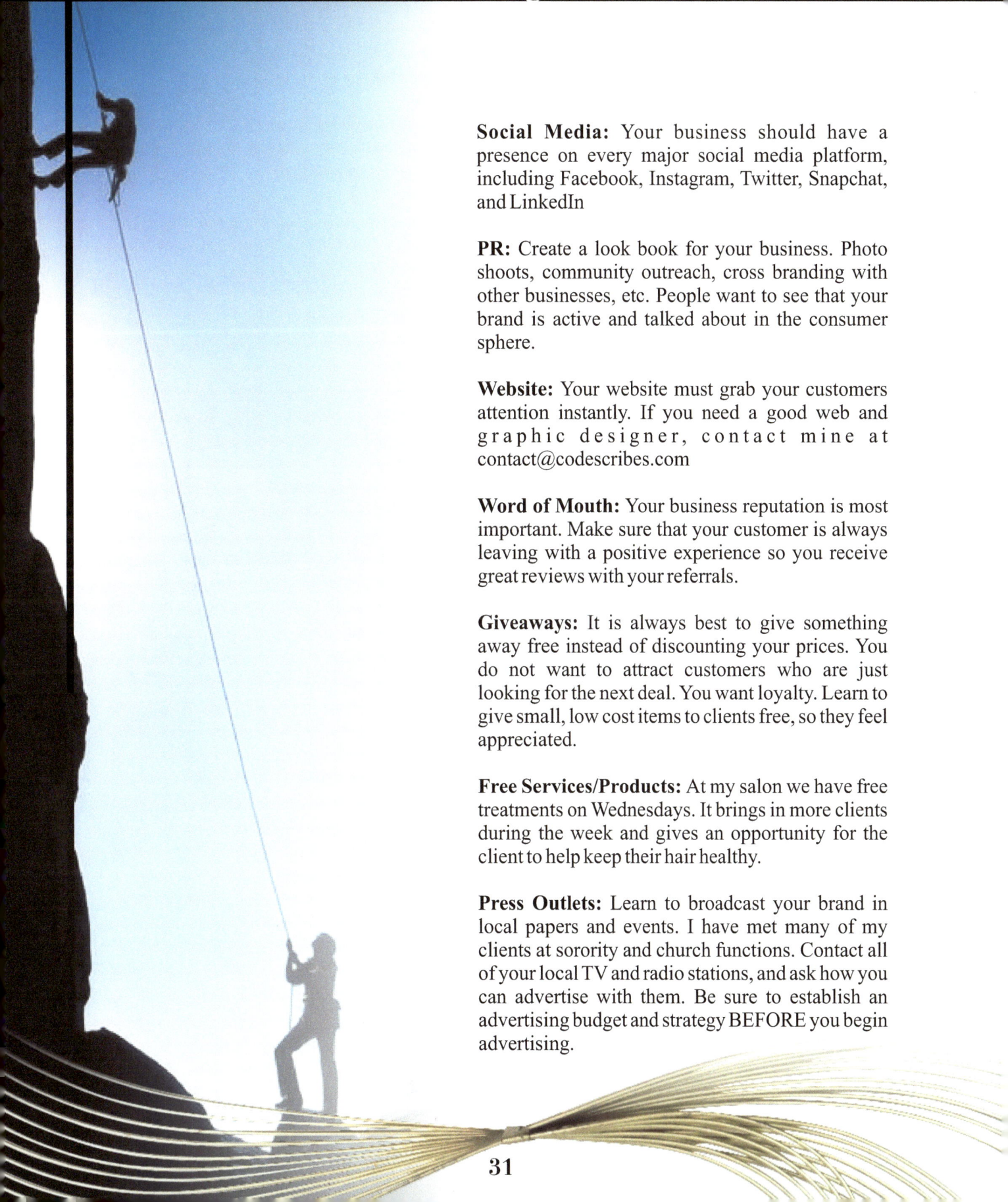

Social Media: Your business should have a presence on every major social media platform, including Facebook, Instagram, Twitter, Snapchat, and LinkedIn

PR: Create a look book for your business. Photo shoots, community outreach, cross branding with other businesses, etc. People want to see that your brand is active and talked about in the consumer sphere.

Website: Your website must grab your customers attention instantly. If you need a good web and graphic designer, contact mine at contact@codescribes.com

Word of Mouth: Your business reputation is most important. Make sure that your customer is always leaving with a positive experience so you receive great reviews with your referrals.

Giveaways: It is always best to give something away free instead of discounting your prices. You do not want to attract customers who are just looking for the next deal. You want loyalty. Learn to give small, low cost items to clients free, so they feel appreciated.

Free Services/Products: At my salon we have free treatments on Wednesdays. It brings in more clients during the week and gives an opportunity for the client to help keep their hair healthy.

Press Outlets: Learn to broadcast your brand in local papers and events. I have met many of my clients at sorority and church functions. Contact all of your local TV and radio stations, and ask how you can advertise with them. Be sure to establish an advertising budget and strategy BEFORE you begin advertising.

There is ALWAYS more than one
way to reach your goal.

REFERENCES

http://www.layrite.com/blog/the-importance-of-attending-hair-industry-events

Excerpt From: Brian Halligan & Dharmesh Shah. "Inbound Marketing, Revised and Updated."

Reading Material

1. Rework by Jason Fried & David Heinemeier Hansson

2. #GIRLBOSS by Sophia Amoruso

3. Brian Halligan & Dharmesh Shah. "Inbound Marketing, Revised and Updated.

4. Jack Canfield "The Success Principles"

5. Micah Wainwright "I Want You To Finance Your Life"

6. Raymond Aaron "Branding Small Business for Dummies"

Products Help List

Richhabits.net
www.Clinkbank.com digital products to promote.
Udemy.com
Kunaki.com (DVD product)
SEO.com White Label
Fiverr.com (make what you like flip it for $5bucks) Constantcontacts.com. To market with clients over email

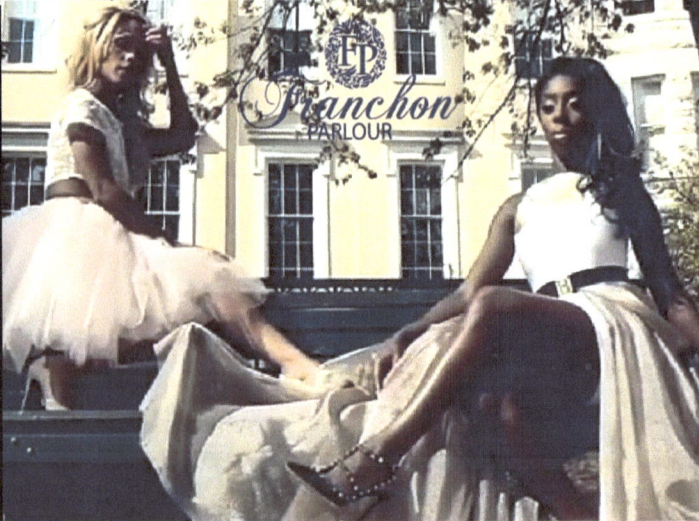